S0-AVG-291

# MARGIT KOVÁCS

PHOTO ALBUM / FOTOALBUM

**PHOTOART** MŰVÉSZETI KIADÓ
Budapest 2001
Collection / Sammlung: Margit-Kovács-Museum  Szentendre
Author / Autor: Lea Schenk
Photography / Foto: Tamás Bakonyi
Photographic portrait of Margit Kovács / Portrait Margit Kovács: André Kertész
Translation / Übersetzung: Aqua Übersetzungsbüro
Pre-print work / Druckvorbereitung: WellCom Grafikstudio
Printing and Binding Typonova Print Shop / Druck: Typonova Druckerei
ISBN 963 00 6484 7

Margit Kovács 1902 – 1977

Margit Kovács, born on November 30, 1902, in Győr, was a masterful ceramist and sculptress known for her love of storytelling. For more than a half a century, she produced innumberable functional objects of unusual beauty and works of fine art on a wide variety of themes, her career ending only with her death on June 4, 1977, in Budapest.

Kovács's pursuits as a ceramist drew upon her experiences as a student of art both in Hungary and abroad. Between 1924 and 1926 she studied graphics at Almos Jaschik's private school, and porcelain painting at the domestic School of Industrial Arts. During the two years that followed, she went on to master the fundamentals of ceramics at the Herta Bücher studio, located in Vienna. She then continued her training on her own at the Staatschule für Angewandte Kunst in Munich, where she also studied plastic modelling as a student of sculpture. It was during the course of a study trip to Copenhagen in 1932 that Kovács first became familiar with the crafting of functional items; in the Sevres Porcelain Factory in 1933, she mastered the technique of modelling with chamotte clay and explored the making of porcelain genre figures. Uniting techniques used to create turned pottery and the more sensitive methods of plastic modelling, Margit Kovács turned her artistry into a series of works which would eventually succeed in bridging the gap between the industrial and fine arts.

Margit Kovács began her career in the early 1930's with the production of modelled terracotta statuettes, reliefs and turned decorative objects. These were followed in the second half of the decade by more stylised murals and individualistic works assimilating folklore motifs. A tendency toward geometric designs also began to figure prominently in her style through her use of turned forms. Small-scale figures formed on the wheel took on simplified conical shapes, while larger works often resembled columns. Kovács adorned her turned figures in decorative ornamentation and gave them a refined finish using both the usual shiny and more experimental matte glazes. In the 1950's, her ceramics, many of which already touched upon the folk and peasant world through numerous and varied genre themes, began to take even deeper inspiration from world folklore, producing boldly turned large-scale figures, statuettes of more realistic tenor, life-like reliefs of epic proportions, and colourful murals. At this point, Kovács moved from terracotta, her favoured material, to chamotte clay and began to explore new themes from the realm of mythology, folktales, and legends, crafting even more expressive figures in ever chunkier forms. The extraordinarily rich fruits of her career, her artistry, emanating both intimacy and a genuine love of the human race, represents a unique voice within contemporary Hungarian ceramic arts.

Margit Kovács ist eine erzählfreudige Schöpferin dekorativer Kunstgegenstände und thematisch unterschiedlicher Gegenstände der bildenden Kunst. Sie wurde am 30. November 1902 in Györ geboren, ihre Schaffensperiode von mehr als einem halben Jahrhundert endete mit ihrem Tod am 4. Juni 1977 in Budapest.

Während ihrer Ausbildung zur Keramikerin durchlief sie verschiedene Schulen im In- und Ausland. In den Jahren 1924-26 studierte sie Grafik an der Privatschule von Álmos Jaschik, und Porzellanmalerei an der Kunsthochschule. Die Grundlagen der Keramik erlernte sie zwischen 1926 und 1928 in Wien in der Keramikwerkstatt von Herta Bücher. Darauf folgte die Weiterbildung zur Keramikerin in München an der Staatsschule für Angewandte Kunst, wo sie auch als Studentin für Bildhauerei die Herstellung von Plastiken erlernte. Ihre Studienreise 1932 führte sie nach Kopenhagen, wo sie sich mit der Gestaltung und Herstellung von Gebrauchsgegenständen beschäftigte, 1933 erlernte sie in der Porzellanmanufaktur von Sevres die Herstellung von Schamottfiguren und die Dekortechnik von Porzellan Genrefiguren. Nach ihrem Studium begann Margit Kovács, durch die einzigartige Zusammenführung der Techniken der Drehscheibe und der Formung von empfindlichen Plastiken, Kunstgegenstände zu schaffen, die die Grenzen zwischen bildender Kunst und traditionellem Kunsthandwerk durchbrachen.

Ihre künstlerische Karriere begann in den frühen Dreißiger Jahren mit der Herstellung von dekorierten Terrakotta Kleinplastiken, Reliefs und gedrehten Ziergegenständen, in der zweiten Hälfte der Dreißiger Jahre begann sie mit der Gestaltung stilisierter Bilder und folkloristisch angehauchter, in ihrer Art einmaliger Ziergegenstände. Die geometrische Tendenz trat bei ihren Figuren durch die angewandte Drehscheibentechnik immer mehr in den Vordergrund. Kleinere Figuren wurden auf eine Kegelform reduziert, größere Figuren hingegen begann sie säulenförmig zu gestalten. Die gedrehten Formen wurden durch Ornamente dekoriert, neben den glänzenden Glasuren experimentierte sie auch mehr und mehr mit Mattglasuren. In den 50er Jahren erreichte ihre folkloristische Inspiration mit den Keramiken der volkstümlich-bäuerlichen Genremotive ihren Höhepunkt. Neben Reliefs und farbigen Wandbildern, die als eine Art lebendes Bild von epischer Erzählung anmuten, gestaltete sie auch realistische Kleinplastiken und auf bravuröse Art gedrehte große Figuren. Den bevorzugten Terrakotta ersetzte sie in den 60er und 70er Jahren durch Schamott, zu dieser Zeit begann sie auch mehrere Themen aus der Mythologie, Märchen und Erzählungen aufzuarbeiten, mit ausdrucksstarkem Dekor oder blockförmiger Gestaltung. Das überaus reiche Lebenswerk von Margit Kovács, mit der empfindsamen, Menschennähe vermittelnden Kunst ist in der neuzeitlichen Keramikkunst einzigartig.

## NURSING MOTHER, 1948
glazed, turned, sculpted terracotta figure, 80 cm

One of Margit Kovács's most endearing themes is that of the Madonna. This particular work is the third such figurine to be imbued with the sculptress's characteristic touch, the first being her Pound-cake Madonna of 1938, a work of folk-baroque effect, followed by the naively sweet and expressively moulded Virgin Swaddling the Child in 1942. While these two previous works portrayed the Madonna standing, the Nursing Mother, a large-scale cloaked figure, gazes out at the observer from a seated position. In this creation, the artist ameliorates the static effect of a symmetric composition taken about a vertical axis by placing the heads of the figures at a gentle tilt. Building her portrayal of the Madonna upon decorative effects, Kovács has brought the most intimate relationship between mother and child to life. Maria's form is framed in an extraordinarily appealing manner by her contoured, blue-trimmed cloak, which is additionally decorated with stylised flowers and spiral motifs.

## STILLENDE MADONNA, 1948
Glasierte, gedrehte, dekorierte Terrakottaplastik 80 cm

Das Lieblingsthema von Margit Kovács ist die Darstellung der Madonna. Vor der Stillenden Madonna hat sie bereits zwei typische Madonnenplastiken geschaffen. 1938 die naive Kegelmadonna, mit ihrer volkstümlich-barocken Kegelform, und 1942 die expressiv dargestellte Wickelnde Madonna. Beide vorhergehenden Madonnenplastiken sind Standbilder, die große, mit Umhang bekleidete Figur der Stillenden Madonna hingegen, sitzt dem Betrachter gegenüber. Die statische Komposition mit Senkrechtachse wird durch die leichte Seitenneigung der Köpfe durchbrochen. Margit Kovács hat mit dieser Figur die intimste Verbindung zwischen Mutter und Kind als Madonnenfigur, aufbauend auf dekorativer Wirkung dargestellt. Die Marienfigur wird durch den wallenden blaugesäumten Umhang mit seinen stilisierten Blumen und Spiralmotiven, auf außergewöhnlich dekorative Art umrahmt

### CUTTING THE LOAF, 1952
glazed, turned figure, 102 cm

Here, Margit Kovács has portrayed a peasant girl cutting a loaf of bread in a boldly turned and sculpted, near life-sized statue. The large-scale turned figure captures this important moment from the life of the Hungarian peasant through the slicing and offering up of a loaf of bread made of wheat flour. The bread, forming the theoretical centre of the composition, symbolises both abundance and well-being. Thus, through the realistic figure of the bread-cutter, Kovács manages to lend the situation an allegorical treatment all her own. The willowy form in peasant costume, her blonde hair caught up in a bun, is an idealised representation of the Hungarian peasant girl. The turned, cylindrical figure is clothed in a dark brown, full-length dress, adorned with blue and white flowers in a decorative design and white trim.

### BROTSCHNEIDER, 1952
Glasierte, gedrehte Figur. 102 cm

Margit Kovács hat das Brot schneidende Bauernmädchen als bravurös gedrehte, fast lebensgroße Figur geschaffen. Mit der großen gedrehten Genrefigur zeigt sie einen wichtigen Moment des ungarischen bäuerlichen Lebens,mit der Darstellung des Aufschneidens und Darbietens von Weizenbrot. Das im Mittelpunkt der Komposition stehende Brot symbolisiert Fülle und Wohlstand. Durch die realistisch geformte Figur der Brotschneiderin kann die Künstlerin so eine einzigartige Symbolik darstellen. In der stehenden schlanken, blonden Gestalt mit bäuerlicher Kleidung stellt Margit Kovács die idealisiserte Figur des ungarischen Bauernmädchens dar. Das bodenlange dunkelbraune Kleid der zylindrisch gedrehten Figur ist mit blau-weißem Dekor und weißem Saum verziert.

## THE BIG FAMILY, 1962
modelled terracotta mural, 110 x 120 cm

Margit Kovács brought her „big family" to life as a large-scale relief of lively composition. The work takes the form, not of a regular quadrilateral, but of a two-dimensional shape of irregular perimeter. The composition is founded upon circular motion, with seated figures forming the waving upper edge of the relief and a bench curved into a half-circle forming its lower rim. The realistic scene depicts the idealised figures of a mother and father together with the forms of their eight children, seated about the table in pairs. Each of the figures has been portrayed dynamically, either linked to its pair as a partner in some action or made to direct a characteristic gesture toward the centre of the composition. The depth of dimension of the relief is emphasised through the beauty of the unglazed terracotta from which it is formed.

## DIE GROßFAMILIE, 1962
Verziertes Terrakotta Wandbild, 110 x 120 cm

Margit Kovács hat ihre „Großfamilie" als monumentales Relief mit bewegter Komposition geformt. Statt der bei Reliefs allgemein vorwiegenden viereckigen Komposition, schuf sie ein Relief unregelmäßiger Form. Die im oberen Bereich der auf Kreisbewegung aufbauenden Komposition sitzenden Figuren bilden den oberen Wellenrand des Reliefs, der untere Teil wird durch eine halbkreisförmige Bank begrenzt. Neben der idealisierten Darstellung von Mutter und Vater sind auf dem realistisch geformten Lebensbild die acht Kinder jeweils paarweise sitzend dargestellt. Die um den kreisförmigen Tisch angeordneten Figuren sind dynamisch geformt: sie sind entweder durch paarweise aufeinander zielende Bewegungen verbunden, oder aber ihre Bewegungen richten sich auf die Mitte der Komposition. Das stark hervorgehobene Relief zeigt die unglasierte Schönheit des Terrakottamaterials.

### IT LOOKS LIKE RAIN, 1953
glazed, turned terracotta figure, 103 cm

This work, another formed on the wheel in boldly monumental proportions, was sculpted one year after the statue Cutting the Bread. The subject, a realistically treated genre figure, sports a dress reflecting that worn everyday by the peasant class. The diagonally arched contour of the dark apron worn over a grey-green dress represents a dynamic detail on the figure's apparel, which otherwise appears reserved, decorated with flowers and tiny white dots. In this work, the subject scans rain clouds in the sky with face turned upward, raising one hand over the brow in a characteristic gesture of blocking the sun's rays. This motion lends the composition its dynamic character, a dynamism further enhanced by the manner in which the figure's torso is rotated in space. The bound-haired peasant girl bears symbolic meaning, as well, her gesture conveying anticipation of supernatural blessing in the form of the rains which will bring fertility to the earth.

### DER REGENBETRACHTER, 1953
Glasierte, gedrehte Terrakottafigur, 103 cm

Margit Kovács schuf diese ebenfalls bravurös geformte, monumentale Figur ein Jahr nach dem „Brotschneider". Das Gewand der Genrefigur in realistischem Stil, spiegelt die alltägliche, bäuerliche Kleidung wider. Ein dynamisches Element der bäuerlichen Kleidung dieser Figur ist die schräg getragene dunkle Schürze über dem grünlich-grauen Gewand, zusätzlich wird diese diskret durch dekorative Blümchen und kleine weiße Punkte verziert. Die Figur, mit ihrem nach Regenwolken Ausschau haltenden, dem Himmel zugewandten Gesicht, hält typisch für den Schutz gegen die Sonne eine Hand über die Augen. Dies verleiht der Komposition der stehenden Figur eine Dynamik, deren Wirkung durch die Drehung des Oberkörpers noch verstärkt wird. Diese den Regen erwartende Bewegung des Bauernmädchens verdeutlicht symbolisch die Erwartung des lebensspendenden Regens, des übernatürlichen Segens.

## PHILEMON AND BAUCIS, 1970
glazed, turned terracotta figure, 70 cm

This turned, cyilindrical figure can be considered one of Margit Kovács's most constructive works. The couple, locked in an intimate embrace, bring one of the tales of Greek mythology to life: the elderly wedded couple, Philemon and Baucis, entertain the god Zeus, who has appeared at their home as a wanderer, seeing to his needs according to their humble means. As a reward, Zeus responds to their wish that they might die together by allowing that they might live on in the form of two trees standing side by side. Kovács depicts the pair not as separate trees, but as one, their heads comprising its two branches. From the cylindrical form of the tree's trunk, only their plastically formed hands rise from the mass of the clay, while all other motifs appear as engraving. That the figures have been turned to living wood is also signified by the brown colour of their faces, necks, and hands. White is the only other colour applied to the decoration of the work.

## PHILEMON UND BAUCIS, 1970
Glasierte, gedrehte Terrakottaplastik, 70 cm

Diese zylindrisch gedrehte Plastik kann als eine der konstruktivsten Werke von Margit Kovács angesehen werden. Das sich innig umarmende Paar verkörpert einen Teil der griechischen Mythologie: das alte Ehepaar Philemon und Baucis bewirtet den als Gast bei ihnen eingekehrten Zeus entsprechend ihrer ärmlichen Möglichkeiten, dieser erfüllt ihnen anschließend  den Wunsch, daß sie beide zur gleichen Zeit sterben mögen und fortan als benachbarte Bäume nebeneinander stehen können. Margit Kovács vereinte die beiden Bäume aus der Mythologie zu einem Stamm, die Köpfe der beiden Figuren entstehen aus den beiden Zweigen dieses Stammes. Aus dem zylindrischen, braunen Stamm heben sich lediglich die Hände plastisch hervor. Alle anderen Ornamente wurden von der Künstlerin eingeritzt. Durch die braune Farbe des Gesichtes, des Halses und der Hände verdeutlicht sie die Umwandlung der Figuren in einen Baum. Außer der braunen Farbe wurde nur wenig Weiß zur Verzierung verwendet.

### From the Family Photo Album, 1953
glazed, turned figure in terracotta, 35 cm

In this piece, a mother and her two children are arranged in a composition of three realistically treated figures. The scene is of waiting for a family photo to be taken. The mother, her blonde hair tied up in a bun, became an idealised genre type of figure in Kovács's repertoire during the 1950's. The female figure with her two children allows us a glimpse of one of the minor events of middle-class life: a family appearing before a photographer for a portrait. The episode is lifted from their everyday life, its nostalgic style imparted through the three charming figures. A small child rests in the lap of a lady in fancy dress, while an older girl leans on her with one elbow. Their garments are finished with both matte engobe glaze and shiny glazes, and display flowered and dotted ornamentation, as well as grid motifs.

### Familienalbum, 1953
Glasierte, gedrehte Terrakottaplastik, 35 cm

Die Mutter und ihre beiden Kinder zeigen in dieser realistischen Dreierkomposition in einer Art Episodenszene, eine Familie, die auf den Fotografen wartet. Margit Kovács zeigt in den fünfziger Jahren die blonde Mutter als idealistische Genrefigur. Die Frauenfigur mit ihren beiden kleinen Kindern stellt die kleinen Geschehnisse der Kleinbürgerlichen Welt dar: die Familie beim Fotografen. Durch die kleinen Figuren zeigt Margit Kovács in nostalgischem Stil diese Episode des täglichen Lebens. Im Schoß der Frau mit ihrem reich verzierten Kleid sitzt das kleinere Kind, das größere Mädchen lehnt sich an sie. Die dekorativen Gewändert verziert außer der matten Engobeglasur noch glänzende Glasur. Neben Blumenornamenten finden wir auf den abwechslungsreichen Gewändern noch Punkte und netzartige Motive.

## DRESSING THE BRIDE, 1953
glazed terracotta mural embedded in cast stone, 102 x 118 cm

The technique of embedding terracotta in cast stone used in Dressing the Bride represents a peculiar experiment on the part of the artist. In the second half of the 1930's, Kovács experimented with arranging pieces of terracotta in a bed of cement to form a mosaic on two occasions (The Last Supper, 1935, and Annunciation, 1938). Both works display an interesting contrast between a homogenous background and the forms which protrude from it. The clay details which make up Dressing the Bride, however, have actually been inlayed in their cast stone bed. This enormous mural shows two girls in folk costume: the sitting figure of a bride in her decorative bridal gown and an attendant who is standing behind in order to straighten her headdress. The stylised stand on which the bride rests bears the inscription of a line from a Hungarian folk song: „I'll be a bride, most beautiful of all."

## SCHMÜCKEN DER BRAUT, 1953
Glasiertes Terrakotta Wandbild in Kunststein 102 x 118 cm

„Schmücken der Braut" ist eine eigenwillige technische Lösung: das Einlegen des Kunstwerkes in Kunststein. In der zweiten Hälfte der Dreißiger Jahre experimentierte Margit Kovács erstmals mit Terrakottateilen, die als Mosaik in Zement eingelegt wurden, bei Werken wie „Das letzte Abendmahl" (1935) oder „Engelsgruß" (1938) erreichte sie damit einen interessanten Kontrast zwischen homogenem Hintergrund und inneren Formen. Bei ihrem Werk „Schmücken der Braut" verwirklichte sie das Einlassen des Lehmausschnittes in Kunststein. Auf dem monumentalen Wandbild sind zwei Mädchen in volkstümlicher Kleidung zu sehen: die sitzende Braut in reichgeschmücktem Brautkleid und Krone, dahinter steht die Dienerin, die den Schmuck richtet. Auf der unter der Braut befindlichen stilisierten Erhöhung ist zu lesen:"Ich bin die Braut, und auch unter den Bräuten die Schönste". Diese Aufschrift zitiert eine, zu diesem Thema gehörende ungarische Volksweise.

· A · Menyasszony · leszek ·
· Annak · is · pedig · tisztelt · leszek ·

## FISHERMEN'S WIVES, 1968
glazed, turned terracotta sculpture, 50 cm

In this sombre composition, five women dressed in dark robes are arranged next to one another in a closed grouping: three in the foreground gazing straight ahead and two behind, with heads turned slightly to one side. The title of the work gives a clue as to the probable object of scrutiny: their forms stand mute upon the banks of the sea, with penetrating eyes and nervous gestures, in order to search for their loved ones in the distance. Each figure in this closed grouping has itself been sculpted as a unique entity. The women's column-like, turned bodies are enveloped in dark brown robes, their folds represented by engraving. The nervous motion of their hands, protruding from within their robes, are the only dynamic element of a composition otherwise imbued with a static and grave tension.

## FISCHERFRAUEN, 1968
Glasierte, gedrehte Terrakottaplastik, 50 cm

Die Komposition strahlt ernste Stimmung aus, fünf dunkel gekleidete Frauen stehen in einer Gruppe zusammen. Hinter den drei dem Betrachter gegenüberstehenden Figuren im Vordergrund, sind noch zwei weitere seitlich Ausschau haltende Figuren zu sehen. Der Name der Komposition gibt bereits einen Hinweis auf den Grund des Ausschauhaltens: die Mitglieder der Gruppe, die nervös gestikulierenden „Fischerfrauen" suchen am Strand wahrscheinlich nach ihren Angehörigen. Nicht nur die Gruppe an sich, sondern die einzelnen Figuren sind in sich geschlossen geformt. Die Falten der dunkelbraunen Gewänder der säulenartig gedrehten Figuren sind eingeritzt. Die einzige dynamische Bewegung bringen die sich aus den dunklen Gewändern hervorhebenden nervös gestikulierenden Hände, ansonsten ist die Komposition statisch und voll ernster Spannung.

### ENGAGED COUPLE AT THE PHOTOGRAPHER, 1953
glazed, turned terracotta sculpture, 48 cm

The two-figure composition of a bridegroom dressed in black with his bride on his arm was sculpted with the type of realism characteristic of Kovács's genre works of the 1950's. The whole of this episode lifted from the everyday life of the middle class, capturing the moment of engagement on film by a photographer, is portrayed with a note of irony. The contrast represented by the black and white of the subjects' dress is supplemented by the use of the colour blue in the ribbon adorning the bride's blonde hair and in the trim of her white dress. Use of both shiny and matte glaze helps to enhance the laciness of the bride's dress. The bride holds white flowers in her hand, and white flowers adorn the groom's jacket, as well. The high-stepping, white-gloved, moustachioed groom and charming, smiling bride belong to the ranks of Margit Kovács's pleasantly ironic characters.

### BRAUTPAAR BEIM FOTOGRAFEN, 1953
Glasierte, gedrehte Terrakottaplastik, 48 cm

Die Komposition des schwarzgekleideten Bräutigams und der sich unterhakenden Braut ist ein Werk in realistischem Stil, der charakteristisch für die Genrewerke von Margit Kovács in den fünfziger Jahren ist. Diese Episode zeigt ein aus dem täglichen Leben der kleinbürgerlichen Welt hervorstechendes Ereignis, die Verlobung, das beim Fotografen festgehalten wird, die ganze Komposition hat einen ironischen Unterton. Der Kontrast der Festtagskleidung schwarz und weiß wird durch das Blau der Schleifen in ihrem blonden Haar und am Saum des weißen Kleides ergänzt. Die Verwendung glänzender und matter Glasuren hebt die Wirkung von Spitze an dem Brautkleid hervor. Die Braut hält in der dem Bräutigam untergehakten Hand weiße Blumen, und auch der schwarze Anzug des Bräutigams ist mit weißen Blumen verziert. Die aufrechte Gestalt des bärtigen Bräutigams mit weißen Handschuhen und die freundlich lächelnde Braut sind freundlich-ironische Figuren von Margit Kovács.

## YOUNG APPRENTICE, 1934
modelled terracotta figure, 115 cm

The beauty of unglazed terracotta gives the standing figure of the Young Apprentice its special appeal. In this sculpture of the early 1930's, measuring in at more than one metre high, Margit Kovács pays tribute to one of the younger characters of the middle-class world. During this period, the sculptress experimented with the modelling of figures in several styles and sizes, resulting in a series of works spanning a whole range of effects, from certain lively genre characters, through the secession-style Woman with Mirror, to Bread Roll Girl, a work linked to the squat forms typical of sculpture dating from the Roman period. Of these, the Young Apprentice seems to be the figure treated with the greatest realism. The static composition of his standing form is made dynamic through his stepping pose, the representation of his arms in mid-motion, and the tilt of his head.

## LEHRJUNGE, 1934
Verzierte Terrakottafigur, 115 cm

Die monumentale Standfigur des Lehrjungen zeigt die unglasierte Schönheit des Terrakotta. In der ersten Hälfte der Dreißiger Jahre erschuf Margit Kovács diese über einen Meter hohe Plastik eines Kindes der kleinbürgerlichen Welt. Sie experimentierte zu Beginn der Dreißiger Jahre mit größeren und kleineren Figuren in verschiedenen Stilformen. Von der in Bewegung befindlichen Genrefigur über das sezessionistisch angehauchte Werk des sich im Spiegel betrachtenden Mädchens, bis hin zu dem im gedrungenen rumänischen Bildhauerstil dargestellten Semmelmädchen. Der Lehrjunge ist im Vergleich zu diesen Werken eine der am realistischsten geformten Figuren. Die statische Komposition der stehenden Figur wird mit ihrer Schrittbewegung und den sich in Bewegung befindlichen Armen, sowie dem geneigten Kopf zur dynamischen Gestalt.

## BIRTH, 1968
modelled sculpture in chamotte clay, 45 cm

The composition in several figures entitled Birth actually constitutes the first piece in a series of three, though it is equally appealing as a separate unit. As part of the triad entitled Birth, Marriage, and Death, it can be interpreted as symbolising but one of three phases of life: Birth presents us with the newborn baby and thus symbolises the commencement of childhood; Marriage follows with its representation of adulthood; finally, Death portrays the conclusion of life in its final phases. Alternately, the three portrayals may be viewed as symbolic representations of past, present, and future. Kovács has given this work a highly unusual composition: the mother lies in a horizontal position, holding her child in her arms, while behind her three female forms stand tall and straight. The combination of horizontal and vertical forms thus lends a peculiar sense of balance to the arrangement. The joy engendered by the presence of the newborn baby is reflected in the three figures that stand behind him in a manner which radiates throughout the entire piece.

## GEBURT, 1968
Verzierte Schamottplastik, 45 cm

Die Komposition aus mehreren Figuren bildet den ersten Teil einer dreiteiligen Reihe, kann jedoch auch als eigenständige Komposition angesehen werden. Wenn wir diese Plastik als Teil der Trilogie Geburt, Ehe und Tod sehen, so kann sie im Rahmen der die drei Lebensstadien symbolisierenden Dreifaltigkeit interpretiert werden: das geborene Kind zeigende Bild der Geburt bedeutet die Kindheit, die Ehe das Erwachsenenalter, der Tod hingegen das Alter. Außer den drei Lebensabschnitten könnte dies auch die Vergangenheit, die Gegenwart und die Zukunft symbolisieren. Die Komposition des Werkes Geburt ist außerordentlich interessant. Im Hintergrund der horizontal liegenden Figur der Mutter, die ihr Kind im Arm hält, stehen drei senkrechte Frauenfiguren, so gleichen sich die waagerechten und senkrechten Richtungen aus. Die Freude über das neugeborene Kind spiegelt sich in einer auf die gesamte Komposition wirkende Weise in den drei Frauen wider.

## APPLE PICKING, 1952
glazed mural on mettlach tiles, 120 x 160 cm

This large-scale decorative mural, depicting a number of figures picking apples, a theme drawn from the everyday life of the Hungarian peasant, conveys a realistic tone through a broad spectrum of colours. The scene portrays four figures in folk costume arranged about a decoratively stylised apple tree, which forms the centre of the composition. In the foreground we see a pony-tailed peasant girl and a young man with a ladder; behind them, in the background, a boy rests in the branches of the trees and a girl with her hair in a bun leans over a basket. The artist places the figures in a peculiar perspective, their horizontal positions with respect to one another in space being conveyed by their vertical placement on the tiles, one above the other. The planar character of the work is enhanced by the manner in which the branches of the apple tree, heavy with leaves and fruit, span the work in an ornamental pattern that blends smoothly with the carpet of flowers below. The rich colours of the piece, painted over a black background, the contrast of red and green patches and the brilliance of its white and yellow, are particularly striking.

## APFELERNTE, 1952
Glasiertes Wandbild auf Mettlacher Platten 120 x 160 cm

Auf dem realistischen monumentalen Wandbild sieht man eine farbenfreudige Komposition. Margit Kovács zeigt hier als Thema der volkstümlichen bäuerlichen Welt die Apfelernte. Im Mittelpunkt der Komposition ein dekorativ stilisierter Apfelbaum, umgeben von vier Figuren in bäuerlichem Gewand: ein Bauernmädchen mit Zöpfen und ein Bursche auf der Leiter im Vordergrund, ein Junge auf der Spitze des Apfelbaumes und ein Bauernmädchen im Hintergrund. Die Künstlerin löst die Perspektivität des Hintereinanderstehens durch übereinander angeordnete Figuren. Die Ebenheit der Komposition wird auch dadurch verstärkt, daß die sich unter der Last der Früchte neigenden Äste mit dem Blumenteppich unter dem Baum ein nahezu zusammenhängendes Ornament bilden. Aus dem Kolorit der farbenfreudigen Komposition mit schwarzem Hintergrund, hebt sich der sich gegenseitig verstärkende Kontrast der roten und grünen Flecken ab, ebenso wie das Strahlen der weißen und gelben Farben.

## BETHLEHEM, 1948
glazed, turned terracotta sculpture, 36 cm

Margit Kovács's nativity scene places the holy family, the Virgin Mary with the baby Jesus seated in her arms and St. Joseph standing beside her, into a tiny stall. The depiction follows the usual iconographical agenda by including the three kings, shepherds, and angels, as well, each occupying its own place within the surrounding natural environment. Thus, in this composition, Kovacs represents the Nativity using differing iconography and a simplified theme. The interior of the tiny arched stall displays woven, raised leaf motifs, fashioned by engraving. The cylindrical forms of the Virgin Mary in her blue dress, baby Jesus in white robe and crown, and St. Joseph in red have been crafted on the wheel. All three figures bear robes decorated with appliqué and rich engraving. The work, which includes elements typical of a baroque-folk style, represents a more intimate tone than is usually encountered in Nativity scenes.

## BETHLEHEM, 1948
Glasierte, gedrehte Terrakottaplastik, 36 cm

Die kleine Bethlehem der Margit Kovács zeigt die Heilige Familie in einer kleinen Nische: Die Jungfrau Maria mit dem Jesuskind auf ihrem Arm, daneben der heilige Josef. Gemäß dem ikongrafischen Programm zeigt die Darstellung Bethlehems neben der in natürlicher Umgebung gezeigten Heiligen Familie auch die Drei Könige, die Schäfer und die Engel. Margit Kovács reduziert in Abweichung von der traditionellen Ikongrafie diese Komposition. Das Innere der kleine Nische mit Bogen ist  mit Motiven aus geritztem Blätterornament netzartig bedeckt. Die Jungfrau Maria in ihrem blauen Gewand, Jesus in weißem Gewand mit Krone und die Figur des heiligen Josef in rotem Gewand sind kegelförmig gedreht. Die Gewänder aller drei Figuren sind mit reichhaltiger aufgelegter und geritzter Verzierung bedeckt. Die Stilelemente des volkstümlichen Barock in dieser Komposition verleihen der Bethlehem Darstellung eine innige Stimmung.

In 1972, in the 70th year of her life, ceramist Margit Kovács donated the greater part of her life's work to the Pest County Museums Directorate in Szentendre. The Vastagh family dwelling in Vastagh György utca (Street) was selected as a site for the museum which would house these works, and in 1973 the permanent exhibition was opened to the public as the Margit Kovács Collection.

In the 18th century the historic building at Vastagh György u. 1 had served as a salt house, where foreign merchants paid a customs duty in salt in exchange for the right to trade. Later, during the times of mail delivered by horse, it was used as the city post office. Later still, it served as a commercial establishment and, finally, was purchased by the Vastagh family. Subsequently, the city named the street where the dwelling is located after the painter György Vastagh (1834-1922), a relative of Béla Vastagh, the member of the Vastagh family most clearly associated with the city of Szentendre.

When the building in Vastagh György utca was renovated for its new role as a museum, Margit Kovács's relief entitled *Boy at the Potter's Wheel (1929)* was placed beside its baroque entranceway. The museum, with its gabled facade, was opened in 1973 with a total floor space of 250 m2. In 1977 the facility was expanded to include a building in its courtyard, adding 300 m2 to the layout. The two separate wings were then joined by opening 9 rooms of various sizes in the lower area of the cellar and a gallery on the first floor. The rooms on the ground floor house primarily functional works of art, along with statues, reliefs and murals from various periods of the artist's career. Located in the enormous, old, staved-ceilinged cellar is an exhibit consisting in large part of works completed in the 30's and 40's. In the newer, upper wing of the cellar, a selection of functional pieces, pitchers, dishes, and figurative, decorative objects can be seen. A tribute to the artist herself, comprised of furniture and other objects from her home, along with an exhibit of documentary photographic material, can be found in the interior of the gallery upstairs.

– · –

1972, in ihrem 70. Lebensjahr überließ Margit Kovács den Großteil ihres Lebenswerkes der Museumsdirektion des Komitats Pest in Szentendre. Als künftiges Museum entschied man sich das Haus der Familie Vastag in der Vastagh György u. in Szentendre einzurichten, und 1973 wurde die ständige Ausstellung eröffnet.

Das unter Denkmalschutz stehende Gebäude Nr. 1 in der Vastagh György u. war im 18. Jahrhundert ein Salzhaus. Die Händler bezahlten hier ihre Zölle in Form von Salz, um Handelsrechte zu erwerben. Später zur Zeit der Pferdepost war dies ein Postamt, wurde dann zu einem Handelshaus und geriet in den Besitz der Vastagh Familie. Die Straße erhielt ihren Namen durch einen Verwandten des in Szentendre lebenden Béla Vastagh, den Maler György Vastagh (1834-1922).

Beim Umbau des Gebäudes zum Museum, fand neben dem barocken Tor an der Hauptfront des Hauses das Scheibenrelief von Margit Kovács aus dem Jahre 1929 seinen Platz. Das 1973 mit 250 m² Ausstellungsfläche eröffnete Museum wurde 1977 auf 300 m² (mit Gebäude im Innenhof) erweitert, und die beiden eigenständigen Gebäudeteile wurden durch einen Kellergang verbunden, somit bilden die neun unterschiedlich großen Räume und die Galerie eine Einheit. In den Räumen im Erdgeschoss finden wir Kunstgewerbliche Gegenstände, sowie Plastiken aus den verschiedenen Stilepochen der Künstlerin, Reliefs und Wandbilder. Auf der größten Fläche, dem Kellergeschoss sind Werke aus den Dreißiger und Vierziger Jahren zu sehen. In dem erhöhten Kellerteil findet der Besucher vorwiegend die Gebrauchsgegenstände der Künstlerin, Krüge, Schalen, und figürliche Ziergegenstände. Im Inneren der Stockwerksgalerie sind Möbel und Gegenstände aus dem Heim der Künstlerin ausgestellt, sowie eine Fotodokumentation zum Gedenken an die Künstlerin.